CONTENTS

A Bell	5
Christmas Elves	6
The Christmas Angel	7
Nazareth Town	9
A Christmas Masque	11
A Song for Christmas Morning	13
The Christmas Minstrel	15
Twelfth Night Song	17
Yule at Thengelfor	18
A Yule-Tide Carol	21
Ballad of the Eve of Yule	23
The Hanging of the Holly	26
The Maid of Bethlehem	27
The Christmas Almsman	29
The Bells of Christmas	31
Christmas Ingle Song	33
Neil MacDonald	35
The Star of Bethlehem	37
Pierol's Christmas	38
Song for the Eve of Yule	40
The Three Kings	42
The Wise Men	44
A Yule Song	46
The Christmas Hunter	47
A Christmas Song	49
A Lover to His Rhyme	51
The Christmas Pilgrimage	53
The Yule-Log	56
Ballad of the Christmas Tryst	58
A Knight's Christmas	62
The White Ladye	63
The Wizard People	65
Holly Song	67
Gennesar	68
Firelight	69

Mother-of-Pearl	70
The Bells of Ardo	71
In the Age of the Year	74
A Lover's Christmas	75
Ballad of Kirkland Hills	76
The Closed Room	78
Under the Holly Bough	80
Cosette's Christmas	82
Pilgrims	86

A BELL

Had I the power
    To cast a bell that should from some grand tower,
    At the first Christmas hour,
  Out-ring,
And fling
A jubilant message wide,
The forgèd metals should be thus allied;—
No iron Pride,
But soft Humility and rich-veined Hope
Cleft from a sunny slope,
And there should be
White Charity,
And silvery Love, that knows nor Doubt nor Fear,
To make the peal more clear;
And then, to firmly fix the fine alloy,
There should be Joy!

CHRISTMAS ELVES

If you walk on Christmas eve,
      And the moon doth shine aright,
    You will see them weave,—
  Nimble gnome, and fay and sprite,—
Devious dances in the lustrous lunar light.
Round and round the holly bole
  Will they dart and glide and spring;
And a tripping troll
  Will they in a chorus sing;
    Threading now in broken, now in linkèd ring.
      Berry bright, berry bright,
        Be the love about your hearth!
      Leafy green, leafy green,
        Be perennial your mirth!
        Sturdy as a holly bole be your footing of the earth!
These white spirits of old Yule,
  Happy you who hear their tune!
Joy with you shall rule,
  Life for you shall be a boon
  Round the year through all the watches of the moon!

THE CHRISTMAS ANGEL

In middle heaven a form behold;
    Fair-aureoled
    Her shapely brow with noon-bright gold;
      Soli Deo Gloria!

Upon a little cloud she stands,
Within her hands
A tympanum with scarlet bands;
      Soli Deo Gloria!

Thereon she playeth without fault,
While up the vault
Her voice makes silvery assault—
      Soli Deo Gloria!

Till, blended with her soaring notes,
Adown there floats
An echo from a myriad throats—
      Soli Deo Gloria!

THE CHRISTMAS ANGEL

An angel she of God's own choir,
Whose one desire
Is higher yet to chant, and higher—
    Soli Deo Gloria!

And every year, upon the morn
When Christ was born
Within the manger-bed forlorn—
    Soli Deo Gloria!

'Tis hers to bid song's raptures run
From sun to sun,
And list to earth's low antiphon—
    Soli Deo Gloria!

Would that our praise might swell and rise
Along the skies,
And scale the gates of Paradise—
    Soli Deo Gloria!

Bearing, with more complete accord,
Unto the Lord,—
Forevermore our watch and ward,—
Soli Deo Gloria!

NAZARETH TOWN

Nazareth town in Galilee!
    Set where the paths lead up from the sea
    That like the chords of a mighty lyre
Dirges over the rocks of Tyre,
Mourns where the piers of Sidon shone,
And the battlements cinctured Ascalon.
They have waned as the sunset wanes;
Little more than a name remains;
But more than a name we hold it,—we,—
Nazareth town in Galilee!

Nazareth town in Galilee!
Ah, what a golden harmony
The dawn seems, flooding its bright white walls!
And, when the violet twilight falls,
What a vast processional of stars
Pageants over its stilled bazaars!
And when the full moon touches the height
Of Tabor, a torch of brilliant light,
Never was sight more fair to see;—
Nazareth town in Galilee!

NAZARETH TOWN

Nazareth town in Galilee!
Strumming a desert melody,
The Bedouin minstrel trolls in the street;
At the Well of the Virgin the maidens meet;
The cactus-hedges crimson to flower,
And the olives silver hour by hour
As through their branches the south wind steals;
A clear bell peals, and a vulture wheels
Over the crest where the wild crags be;—
Nazareth town in Galilee!

Nazareth town in Galilee!
At the sound of the words how memory
Kindles as earth does under the spring,
Till the dead days rise for our visioning;
And out of them one compassionate face
Beams with a more than mortal grace;
Out of them one inspiring voice
Cries in the ears of the world "rejoice!"
And ever a beacon of hope shall be
Nazareth town in Galilee!

A CHRISTMAS MASQUE

FIRST KING

I am the monarch Melchior,
    Mighty alike in peace and war.

SECOND KING

I am the sovereign Balthasar;
A myriad fold my liegemen are.

THIRD KING

The royal ruler Jasper, I,
Lord of a spacious empery.

FIRST KING

Yet do I seek a little child,—

A CHRISTMAS MASQUE

SECOND KING

A tiny nursling undefiled;

THIRD KING

And I am one likewise beguiled.

FIRST KING

To Him whose coming stars foretold,—
A babe divine in mortal mould,—
I bear this goodly gift of gold.

SECOND KING

To Him whose life shall ease the sting
Of mankind's weary travailing,
This fragrant frankincense I bring.

THIRD KING

To Him whose loving words shall stir
To aspirations holier,
My offering is this precious myrrh.

ALL

Piercing the mists of time, we see
The cruel cross, the agony,
And, whelmed with pity, bend the knee.
Piercing the mists of time, we gaze
Adown the future's opening ways,
And hear the swelling prayer and praise.
Piercing the mists of time, we hail
The day when woe and sin shall fail,
And over all His love prevail.

A SONG FOR CHRISTMAS MORNING

O wear for garment mirth
      Upon the soul,
    As all the fields of earth
  Wear one white stole!
A dream of things long gone
    Let sorrow be:
Turn thou thine eyes on dawn,
    Thy heart on glee!

What wonder everywhere
    Above, abroad!
The amplitudes of air
    Abrim with God.
His presence shining through
    The risen sun,
And in the bending blue
    His benison.

A SONG FOR CHRISTMAS MORNING

Into the gulfs of gloom
     Go death and night;
Behold around thee bloom
     Glad life and light!
The veil of darkness drawn,
     Thy vision free,
Turn thou thy soul on dawn,
     Exultingly!

THE CHRISTMAS MINSTREL

N ow that the joy-day of the year is nearing,
    In that fair sun-land set 'twixt sea and sea,
    From hill and mountain dale behold appearing
With jocund strains a minstrel company.

The reeds that shepherds played in eras olden,
    These are the tuneful pipes whereon they blow;
The sky that over-arches is the golden,
    The bright Calabrian sky of long ago.

And since the decades of the saints and sages,
    When here to Christ was first raised prayerful praise,
These minstrel men through all the echoing ages
    Have heralded the hallowed Christmas days.

From lonely shrines on steep and stony byways
    Their clear wild music up the pathway soars;
It gushes like a fount on traveled highways,
    And through the populous piazza pours.

THE CHRISTMAS MINSTREL

They cling to their old ways, these simple-hearted
    And humble dwellers on the uplands high;
Their notes, an echo of the days departed,
    Span gulfs of time, and bring the dead years nigh.

Long may the cool Calabrian laurel alleys
    Hearken the strains, in rarer ether born,
Of minstrels wending down the mountain valleys
    To greet the coming of the Christmas morn!

TWELFTH NIGHT SONG

Heaped be the fagots high,
      And the half-burnèd bough
      From last year's revelry
    Be litten now!
Brimmed be the posset bowl
For every lusty soul;
    And while the maskers rule,
    Cry 'Noel!' cry 'Noel!' down all the halls of Yule!

O eager viols, thrill!
    Pipe, hautboys, clear and sweet!
Work your impetuous will,
    Ye restless feet!
For every lip—a glass!
For every lad—a lass!
    And, ere the ardors cool,
    Cry 'Noel!' cry 'Noel!' down all the halls of Yule!

YULE AT THENGELFOR

It was Yule at Thengelfor,—
The sharp white tide of Yule;
And the mailèd Thanes of War,
Bred in the fiery school
Of the devotees of Thor,
Flung into the council-hall
With sneer and clamorous call
At the calm-browed Thanes of Peace
Who worshiped without cease,—
Bending in prayer the knee
To the One of Galilee
Who died, as they said, for all.

Each man stood in his place
That sharp white noon of Yule,
And the War-Thanes hooted "fool,"
And "coward" and "craven knave;"
And they flashed, each one, a glaive
In every Peace-Thane's face.
But the Peace-Thanes were not cowed,
Smiling their quiet smile

YULE AT THENGELFOR

At the flaunts and threats and jeers
Roaring about their ears;

And they held them poised and proud,
Till, after a breathing while,
The tumult died like the sea
Subsiding sullenly
Around the breast of an isle
Set at the last fiord's verge,
Fronting the western surge.

Then into the council-hall
Where Peace confronted War,—
Where Christ confronted Thor,—
Dauntless, willowy, tall,
Came a maid of Thengelfor,—
The Princess. Ah, how fair
Was the sunrise sheen of her hair,
More wondrous to behold
Than her coronet of gold!
And she paused between them there,
As white as the Yule was white,
Till a hush fell on the air
Like the hush of the middle night.
And she said, "What stand ye for?"
To the mailèd Thanes of War;
And they shouted shrill, "For Thor,
And the kingdom's olden might!"
Then she turned her, level-eyed,
To the Peace-Thanes. "Ye?" she cried;
As in one voice they replied,
"For Christ, and the rule of right!"

"Thor and the war and might!"
Thus she mused for a space;
"Christ and peace and the right!"
And a glory mantled her face.

YULE AT THENGELFOR

"Better the right than might,
Ye valiant Thanes of War!
Blood now the Yule is white?
Nay, 'twere a grievous sight!—
Better the Christ than Thor!"

And ever and evermore
By the Baltic's rugged shore,
In the halls of Thengelfor,
Right not might is the rule,
The Christ and not sanguine Thor
At the sharp white tide of Yule!

A YULE-TIDE CAROL

O lightly lift thy finger,
  Thou loving lutanist,
 And let around us linger
Thy music's mellow mist!
Aye, let the strain beat faster
 In captivating time,
And mirth shall be our master
 Until the midnight chime!

 Noel!—hang high the holly
  While leaps the Yule-log's light;
 We'll drive gray Melancholy
  Abroad into the night!

With silvery touch and tingle,
 Like brooks 'twixt sunny swards,
Each soaring voice shall mingle
 And marry with the chords;
So shall the liquid laughter
 Of mirth and music rule,

A YULE-TIDE CAROL

Till rings the roof-tree's rafter
    With revelries of Yule.

      Noel!—hang high the holly,
         And twine the ivy-tod;
      My merries, we'll be jolly,
         And spurn care like a clod!

BALLAD OF THE EVE OF YULE

It was hard on the tide of Yule,
 And the wind bit shrewd and sharp,
 Churning the river pool,
And turning the deep-wood boughs,
 That were wont to droop and drowse,
To the moaning strings of a harp.

A snow-threat gloomed the sky,
 And with iterant, raucous caw
A bevy of rooks went by,
 Each a seeming thing
 Of evil, ominous wing
Flapping adown the flaw.

Then night fell over the fen,
 And he mused, still stumbling on,
"Out of the world of men
 Into the shades I go!"
 And he grimly laughed, when lo,
A light on his pathway shone!

BALLAD OF THE EVE OF YULE

"Mine enemy's tower!" he said,
     As the beacon beckoned him. "Well,
Succor were likely as bread
     To be had from a shard or stone,
     Or meat from a wolf-gnawed bone,
Or hope in the heart of hell!"

Yet he steered him sheer on the flare,
     With a "Here or there, 'tis one!
A corpse in the morning air,
     Frozen as rigid as steel,
     Or a form on gibbet or wheel,—
What matters it how 'tis done!"

He clanged a summons clear,
     Keeping his grip on hate;
And he wavered not to hear
     A word from a tongue abhorred,—
     Then back swung the outer ward,
And his enemy stood in the gate.

Eyes upon burning eyes
     Hung, as when war-fires rule
Under the angry skies;
     Then, ere the wrath-flame died,
     "Welcome!" his enemy cried,
"For this is the eve of Yule."

Into the banquet-hall
     He was bid as a chosen guest;
And there before them all
     Did his enemy give him meat,
     And bread of the finest wheat,
And golden wine of the best.

BALLAD OF THE EVE OF YULE

Then was he brought to a room
    Where rugs were soft on the floor,
And a fire made fair the gloom;
    And, warned with a stern behest
    Of the sacred rights of a guest,
A guard was set at the door.

Through the black night-watches long
    Did he wait on sleep, but when
Came the peal of the matin song
    No slumber had kissed his brow;
    So he girded himself, for now
The sunlight lay on the fen.

Then once more did his foe
    Proffer him drink and food;
Forth to the court below
    Did his enemy lead the way,
    Where, as one for a fray,
Chafing, a charger stood.

"Hate!—it is burned into shame;
    Scorn!—of myself is the scorn;
Blame!—I confess to the blame;
    Vengeance is thine!" he said,
    And with averted head
He rode out into the morn.

THE HANGING OF THE HOLLY

The holly is for happiness;
    Hang it, hang it high,
    When the holy morn we bless
Shows its rose along the sky!

The holly is for heartsome cheer;
    Hang it, hang it high,
While the glory of the year
    Lights the heights of all the sky!

The holly is for home-side mirth;
    Hang it, hang it high,
Till the dearest day of earth
    Fades in shades along the sky!

THE MAID OF BETHLEHEM

It was a maid of Bethlehem;—
  As fair as spring was she
  When first lifts up its fragile cup
  The rathe anemone.

It was a man of Bethlehem;—
  As dark of heart was he
As is night's Stygian shadow cast
  Upon the lone Dead Sea.

He fawned where'er she set her foot,
  He followed her like fate;
And when she sealed his lips with scorn,
  He held a tryst with hate.

And then, as venom through the veins,
  Through Bethlehem there ran
A whispered malice in the air
  That spread from man to man.

THE MAID OF BETHLEHEM

"And shall this living lie endure?"
        In rising rage, they said;
"The purging fire shall work a cure
        Upon her sinful head!"

It was the maid of Bethlehem,
        In all her stainless grace,
They seized before the House of God
        Within the market-place.

It was the man of Bethlehem
        Who led the throng elate
That bore her out with mocking shout
        Beyond the city gate.

Around her heaped they fagots high,
        And touched the pile with flame;
"Behold!" they cried, "the wanton witch!
        She expiates her shame!"

"O sinless One of Calvary,"
        Then did they hear her say,
"Prove Thou my blameless innocence
        On this, Thy natal day!"

Lo, as she spake, each fiery tongue
        Leaped on her foe of foes,
The while from charred and smoking boughs
        Burst rose on crimson rose!

It was the man of Bethlehem
        Who died in agony;
It was the maid of Bethlehem
        Who went unharmed and free.

THE CHRISTMAS ALMSMAN

I t was a Christmas almsman
    Came to a palace door;
    The flambeaux flared, the music blared,
    And gleamed the waxen floor.

"Out on thee, for a vagrant!"
    A pompous porter cried;
Quick, get thee gone ere goads be drawn
    To scourge thy tattered hide!"

The mirth roared to the rafter,
    With plenty groaned the board,
Yet naught they gave that almsman gaunt
Save flaunting fleer and ribald taunt,
Despite his bare and bitter want,
    From all their Yule-tide hoard!

It was a Christmas almsman
    Unto a hovel came;
The walls so grim were drear and dim
    With one pale candle flame.

THE CHRISTMAS ALMSMAN

Yet spake the kindly hoveler
    Who saw the beggar's face:
"You're welcome here, though lean our cheer;
    Enter, and bide a space!"

He shambled in; he crouched him down;
    He ate their meagre fare;
And lo, they found, when he had sped,
A scrip of gold and jewels red!
The hoveler had housed and fed
    An angel unaware!

THE BELLS OF CHRISTMAS

"Pilgrim, you of the loosened lachet,
What do you hear as you roam and roam?"
"Master, I list to the bells of Christmas,
The bells of Christmas, calling me home!

"They call and call, and I fain would hasten
Back to the warmth of the old roof-tree,
To the plentiful board and the merry faces,
And the twilight prayer at the mother's knee!"

"Pilgrim, you of the loosened lachet,
Why, then, still do you roam and roam?"
"Master, 'twas but a dream they conjured,
The bells of Christmas, calling me home.

"'Twas but a vision out of the distance,
Happy and holy and sweet, forsooth!
'Twas but a vision out of the distance,
Out of the long lost vale of Youth!"

THE BELLS OF CHRISTMAS

"Pilgrim, you of the loosened lachet,
    All of us have our dreams like thee,
And back are borne by the bells of Christmas
    To the twilight prayer at the mother's knee!"

CHRISTMAS INGLE SONG

Now once more the year has run
    (Sun succeeding sceptred sun)
      To the time of hallowed birth,
To the holiest tide of earth;
Out with sadness! out with sin!
Let us hail the Christ-Child in!

While we lift our thanks for thrift,
Praise the giver and the gift,
With the holly, berried bright,
Druid ivy sprays unite!—
Long they both have sacred been;
Let us hail the Christ-Child in!

And the back-log,—let it be
From some ancient forest tree
Great of girth, that flames may roar
Up the chimney high and hoar,
Thus to swell our merry din;
Let us hail the Christ-Child in!

CHRISTMAS INGLE SONG

Far into the night with song
Let us the old rites prolong!
Cry, "Noel! noel! noel!"
Until peals the midnight bell!
If we peace and love would win,
Let us hail the Christ-Child in!

NEIL MACDONALD

"Whither away, O Neil MacDonald?
         Whither away so fleet hie ye?"
    "I have a tryst to keep, my mother,
    Under the boughs of the holly tree!"

"Go ye not, O Neil MacDonald!
         Go ye not, prithee! prithee!"
"I must keep the tryst, my mother,
         Under the boughs of the holly tree!"

Into the night leaps Neil MacDonald;
         Every man has a weird to dree;
He will dree his weird this Yule-tide
         Under the boughs of the holly tree.

In the north the pale auroras
         Flash and waver spectrally;
But the purple shadows slumber
         Under the boughs of the holly tree.

NEIL MACDONALD

Over the burn bounds Neil MacDonald;
    Through the bracken plunges he;
He has won to the purple shadows
    Under the boughs of the holly tree.

"O my love!" cries Neil MacDonald;
    "O my love! my love!" cries she;
And their lips are met together
    Under the boughs of the holly tree.

Bitter the frost upon the moor-side,
    Bitter the frost, but what recks he,
With his arms about Fiorna
    Under the boughs of the holly tree!

"What is that I hear, beloved?
    What is that dark shape I see?"
"You but dream, my Neil MacDonald,
    Under the boughs of the holly tree."

"He dreams not, your Neil MacDonald,
    Sister, false as the falsest be!"
Hark!—the clan-call of MacGregor
    Under the boughs of the holly tree!

Hark!—the clan-call of MacGregor!—
    Every man has a weird to dree!
He has dreed his, Neil MacDonald,
    Under the boughs of the holly tree.

THE STAR OF BETHLEHEM

O ut of the past's black night
　　　There shines one star
　　Whose light
Is more than countless constellations are.

High in the east it gleams;—
　　This radiant star
Whose beams
　　Are more to man than all the planets are.

Still be thy light displayed,
　　O Bethlehem star,
Nor fade
　　Until the circling systems no more are!

PIEROL'S CHRISTMAS

Into the hall on the night of Yule
　　　Capered the jester, blithe Pierol,
　　Crying merrily, "Gifts for a fool!"
　　　Sooth, right well did he play the role,
　　　Though the wolf of bitterness gnawed his soul!

Proud his birth as the proudest there,—
　　　Count or baron or haughty knight,
　　But poverty was his sorry share,—
　　　A lonely tower on a barren height
　　　(And a wit as bright as his purse was light).

So under the motley he hid his name;
　　　Under the motley he hid his heart;
　　But he could not hide nor he could not tame
　　　His leaping spirit that would out-start,
　　　Nor his face,—Endymion's counterpart.

PIEROL'S CHRISTMAS

"Gifts for a fool!" Troth, they loved him well,—
    Loved his beauty and blithesomeness,
Loved his quips and lyric spell
    Of the songs he sang with so gay a stress,
    And his head thrown back like a hawk in jess!

So they tossed him,—this one a golden chain,
    That one a bracelet, another a ring;
Till out of all of that feasting train
    There was only a maid who had failed to fling
    Some bauble to him,—some costly thing.

And she,—how fair like the thorn in May
    She seemed as she sat in her stainless guise!—
As he paused in his pirouetting gay,
    Caught to heart the look in his fearless eyes
    That were fixed upon her in yearning wise;

And raising a hand,—ne'er was shapelier
    By prince or paladin won, I wis,
In the shock of the lists, or the silken stir
    Of the courts of Love who is queen of bliss!—
    She cast him the honeyed boon of a kiss.

"Gifts—for a—fool!" far, fainter the cry
    Drooped in the distance to quaver and shift,
A moment to linger, and then to die.
    Of all that meed of a jester's thrift
    Which to Pierol was the dearest gift?

SONG FOR THE EVE
OF YULE

Here's a fig for Melancholy,
      Now the year is at the Yule!
    Welcome Fun and welcome Folly!
    Welcome anything that's jolly!
What say you, sweet Mistress Molly,
      Shall not Love and Laughter rule?

Come and close about the ingle
      While the caverned chimney roars!
Song and merriment shall mingle
Till the very rafters tingle;
Then shall sound the jangle-jingle
      Of the sleigh-bells at the doors!

Out upon all frowning faces!
      Out upon the ghost of Gloom!
In with games and glees and graces!
Loose (for once) smug Custom's traces;
Put old Momus through his paces!
      Give the merry maskers room!

SONG FOR THE EVE OF YULE

Aye, a fig for Melancholy!
    Garland Love, let Laughter rule!
Hail to Fun and hail to Folly!
Hail the jovial and the jolly!
Shall we not, sweet Mistress Molly,
    Now the year is at the Yule!

THE THREE KINGS

Came those monarchs, grave and hoar,
  With their gifts, a goodly store,
   Gold and frankincense and myrrh,
On that holy night of yore,—

Ator, Sator, Sarasin,
In their hallowed purpose kin,
  Following the guiding star,
Each a sacred goal to win.

Did they bear their offerings,
Such a wealth of precious things,
  Unto one of princely place,
Sprung, like them, from earthly kings?

Nay, but to an infant born
In a lowly spot forlorn
  Yet around whose glorious face
Shone a halo like the morn!

THE THREE KINGS

For a spirit unto each
Spake in no uncertain speech,
      Saying, "In a manger lies
One who God to man shall teach;

One who shall the night o'erthrow,
Bearing heaven with Him below,—
      Love that triumphs over hate,
Peace and joy that conquer woe."

So those monarchs, men of fame,
Bowed before Him, blessed His name,
      Laid their offerings at His feet,
Passed as swiftly as they came.

Stretch the years, a checkered chart,
Since they played their deathless part,
      Yet to-day may we, like them,
Giving, hold the Christ at heart.

THE WISE MEN

The Wise Men wander across the wold,
(O the Star in the sky!)
Bearing their goodly gifts of gold.
(How the low wind whispereth by!
Whispereth
Of birth, not death,
With joy in its lifted cry!)

The Wise Men come unto Bethlehem;
(O the Star in the sky!)
A star is the beacon that guideth them.
(How the soft wind hasteneth by!
Hasteneth
The while it saith,
"O the Light of the World is nigh!")

THE WISE MEN

The Wise Men kneel at the infant's feet,
    (O the Star in the sky!)
And the loving mother smileth sweet.
      (While the wind it hurrieth by,—
          Hurrieth
          As it gladly saith,
     "O the Hope of the World is high!")

The Wise Men rise, and they go their ways;
    (O the Star in the sky!)
And all this happened in the ancient days.
      (But the wind still gladdeneth by,—
          Gladdeneth
          At the death of Death,
     That Life hath the victory!)

A YULE SONG

Who cries 'tis folly to wreathe the bright holly?
      Who is it scoffs at the mistletoe bough?
    Marry, then, out on him! marry, then, flout on him!
    If there's a time to be jolly, 'tis now!

Berry-tide, cherry-tide, each is a merry tide,
    And there's charm in the nutting, I vow!
But none surpasses,—how say you, my lasses?—
    The time for up-hanging the mistletoe bough!

Reason,—away with it! Men have grown gray with it,
    Pondering why and considering how;
We have no part in it,—nay, and no heart in it!—
    Under the droop of the mistletoe bough!

So, lads, your choices all! Lift, maids, your voices all!
    Love levels prince with the man at the plough.
We'll make our boast of it, we'll make our toast of it,—
    Ne'er may it wither, the mistletoe bough!

THE CHRISTMAS HUNTER

With blare of horn and holloa,
　　　Who is it forth doth fare?
It is the Christmas Hunter
　　　Who rides adown the air.

Upon his wild steed, Sleipnir,
　　　He storms across the sky;
And like the moan of ocean
　　　His vanguard surges by.

They are the Judas-hearted,—
　　　They are the souls of them
That spurned God's own anointed,
　　　The Man of Bethlehem.

For them nor peace nor joyance
　　　At this high tide of Yule,
Since they are doomed to follow
　　　The Hunter's iron rule.

THE CHRISTMAS HUNTER

Rage fills his veins with riot
    When peals the Christmas mirth,
For memory bears him backward
    When he had power on earth.

So mad he whirls his minions
    Behind him fast and far,
Without or pause or pity,
    From star to utmost star.

The once almighty Odin
    Whom Christ hurled from his height,
He is the Christmas Hunter
    Who roams the voids of night.

A CHRISTMAS SONG

O'er the wastes the crows are calling—
      Caw! Caw!
    In the hedges of the haw,
Sparrows with their merry clatter
Cheep and chatter,—
Naught's the matter!
Marry, marry! naught's the matter!
       Then it's ho! heigh-ho!
All the waking world's aglow!
And the mirthful bells of Christmas
      Ring across the snow!

Down the garden Colin's calling—
     Mollie! Mollie!
In the thickets of the holly
Choruses the hidden starling,
Saucy darling!
You're behind her!
Kiss her, kiss her, when you find her!

A CHRISTMAS SONG

Then it's ho! heigh-ho!
Who's for worry, who's for woe,
When the wooing bells of Christmas
Ring across the snow?

A LOVER TO HIS RHYME

Go seek her out, my rhyme,
        Her of the cruel heart,
            And with your softest chime,
    And with your blandest art,
Plead that this merry time
        May see her frowns depart.

And whisper, ah, so low!—
        (And mark ye if she sigh!)
That sprays of mistletoe
        Are plucked to hang on high,
That holly berries glow,
        That Christmas-tide is nigh.

And if ye win one smile,
        O speed ye hither swift!
From eyes cast down the while
        The aching gloom will lift,
And in the orchard aisle
        Will flower the frozen drift.

A LOVER TO HIS RHYME

More I that ray will prize
    Than pearls of orient birth;
'Twill set the wintry skies
    A-dazzle over earth;
And love, in lilied guise,
    Will light the Christmas hearth.

THE CHRISTMAS PILGRIMAGE

(BETHLEHEM)

What means this waiting throng?
Whence have these weary, way-worn wanderers come?
Why rises, in strange tongues, the expectant hum,
Like that tense under-song
The joyful Jordan voices in the spring
Till Hermon hearkens, leaning grandly down,
And wearing still his shimmering snowy crown?
Soon will these murmuring lips with ardor sing,
And soon these lifted faces, wan or brown,
Glow into worship that is rapturing.
Back will be thrown the consecrated door,
And then these feet, from many a distant shore,
Be privileged to press the hallowed floor.

Why have they come,—the hardy mountaineer
From Lebanon's cedars and their checkered shade?
The merchant and the snowy-mantled maid
Who hold great Nilus dear?
Why have they come,—the men with restless eyes

53

THE CHRISTMAS PILGRIMAGE

And pallid cheeks that tell of norland skies?
Why have they come,—the Latin and the Greek?
Do pilgrims thus this sanctuary seek
Because 'twas here
For year on fiery year
The red earth drank
The deluged blood of Paynim and of Frank?
Or do they surge to see
The antique symmetry
Of springing arch and carven pillar fine,
In this old holy house of Constantine?

Ah, no! ah, no! To them the memory
Of war is not, and monarchs play no part
In any thought that stirs an eager heart.
They have no eyes to see
A single graceful groining. What care they
If here, upon a bygone Christmas-day,
The King-crusader, Baldwin, took his crown!
Or what to them the saint of blest renown
In yonder sepulchre, now crumbling clay!
Their patient feet one precious spot would press,
Their yearning eyes would lovingly caress
The time-dulled silver star
Sunk deep within the pavement, footfall-worn:
"Here, of the Virgin Mary, Christ was born,"
They read, these pilgrims who have plodded far.
They read and pass and ponder. Few can see
The tiny chapel and the dim-lit shrine,
And feel no thrill, despite the mummery,
Of something more divine
Within the breast than ever pulsed before.
Then let us pilgrims be
Upon this sacred day we all adore!
Although our mortal feet touch not the floor,
Although our mortal eyes may not behold,

THE CHRISTMAS PILGRIMAGE

Our spirits may take flight,
And with immortal sight
Stand where the prayerful wise-men stood of old
In ecstasy of adoration, when
They saw the Savior of the sons of men.

THE YULE-LOG

Hale the Yule-log in!
      Heap the fagots high!
   With a merry din
   Rouse old Revelry!
Cry "Noel! Noel!"
   Till the rafters ring,
And the gleeful bell
   Peals its answering!

Brim the Christmas cup
   From the wassail-bowl,
Now the flame leaps up
   With its ruddy soul!
In the glowing blaze
   How the dancers spin!
Deftest in the maze,
   Nimble Harlequin!

THE YULE-LOG

Grim Snapdragon comes
    With his mimic ire,
And his feast of plums
    Smothered in the fire.
O the days of mirth,
    And the nights akin!
Heap the Christmas hearth;
    Hale the Yule-log in!

BALLAD OF THE CHRISTMAS TRYST

"It's hey! my merry huntsman,
　　　With hound and hawk and horn,
　　Where hie ye to the hunting
　　This crispy Christmas morn?"

"It's ho! mine ancient gossip,
　　To Wildmere wood I go,
To seek beneath the boughs of Yule
　　The roebuck and the roe."

"It's ha! my merry huntsman,
　　A cunning tongue have ye;
With deer ye keep no Christmas tryst
　　Beneath the greenwood-tree."

"It's hist! mine ancient gossip,
　　I prithee, speak me low,
Lest they that love me not should hear
　　To Wildmere wood I go."

BALLAD OF THE CHRISTMAS TRYST

"It's list! my merry huntsman,
        They wot thy coming well,
And wait thee where the pathway dips
        To cross the birken dell."

"It's good! mine ancient gossip,
        How many may there be
Betwixt me and my Christmas tryst
        Beneath the greenwood-tree?"

"It's hark! my merry huntsman,
        There's Bernard of the Bow,
Sir Egbert of the Crooked Arm,
        And Giles of Clariveaux;

"There's Giles, my merry huntsman,
        The wiliest of men,
Brother in blood, though black his heart,
        To one whose name ye ken."

"Gramercy! ancient gossip,
        And shall these stay my foot?
Then may the House of Hardigrave
        Be withered to the root!"

He gave his page his hound in leash,
        His hawk and eke his horn,
And gaily did he onward ride
        Beneath the Christmas morn.

And now the birken dell was won,
        And now the shallow ford,
And now he heard the scabbard ring
        Its answer to the sword.

And forth from out the coppice deep
        Rode Bernard of the Bow,

BALLAD OF THE CHRISTMAS TRYST

Sir Egbert of the Crooked Arm,
    And Giles of Clariveaux.

Small parley was there then, God wot,
    But bickering of steel,
And down clashed Bernard of the Bow
    Beneath his charger's heel.

And Egbert of the Crooked Arm
    Reeled sidewise as he knew
The sharp bite of a falchion's point
    His stricken harness through.

Then clear rang out the huntsman's shout,
    Right merrily cried he,
"God's with the son of Hardigrave
    Who loves *La Belle Marie!*"

Oh, deep cursed Giles of Clariveaux
    To hear his sister's name,
While 'neath his vizor burned his eyes
    Like orbs of evil flame!

"Have at thee, Hardigrave!" he hissed,
    "This riding thou shalt rue!"
And round them like a fiery mist
    The spiteful sparks outflew.

'Twas parry, cut and countercut,
    And fiercer-faced the while
Grew treacherous Giles of Clariveaux
    To mark the huntsman's smile.

And seeing he was sore beset,
    That urgent grew his need,
He aimed a caitiff's coward blow
    To maim his foeman's steed.

BALLAD OF THE CHRISTMAS TRYST

But vain that cruel, craven thrust,
  For whiles he strove to rein
The shoulder of his sword-arm
  Was riven half in twain.

O starling in the thicket, see
  Where, eyes with love aglow,
Adown the forest pathway goes
  The rose of Clariveaux!

And hearken, O ye holly boughs!
  And, O ye larches, list!
It is the song of one who rides
  To keep his Christmas tryst.

A KNIGHT'S CHRISTMAS

I hear the shrilling hautboys sound,
    The thrilling drums take up the din,
    And through the doorway's gaping bound
    A lusty, mincing manikin
    Bears, garlanded, the boar's head in.

The great bells clamor in the tower
    Their jubilation. Down the hall
Mirth bursts into a brilliant flower
    Of quip and toast and madrigal;
    "Noel! Noel! Noel!" cry all.

And yet joy seems a thing foredone
    Forevermore in every place
Beneath the red rays of the sun;—
    What is Christ's mass that wrought man grace
    Without the favor of love's face!

THE WHITE LADYE

"The flax upon your distaff
      Is yellow as your hair,
    But why, on Christmas even,
Thus spin you, maiden fair?

"The joy-bells in the steeples
      Are ringing clear and wide;
O stop the whirring spindle,
      And put the flax aside!"

"Nay, but I may not, master,
      Although I weary be,
Lest through the open shutter
      Should peer the White Ladye;

"And find my treadle idle,
      My flax in tangled fold,
And on the merry morrow
      Forget her gift of gold.

THE WHITE LADYE

"For to the slothful virgin
    She causeth sorrowing,
But to the thrifty maiden
    A blessing she doth bring!"

A soft touch at the shutter,—
    A face divine to see!
It is the fairy spinner,
    It is the White Ladye!

THE WIZARD PEOPLE

Adown the ways of winter,
        Above the vasts of snow,
        With woven flame their sandals shod,
Through airy wastes by paths untrod,
        The wizard people go.

By day their feats are hidden,
        But night beholds their mirth,
When in the abysses of the air
Their sorceries they flaunt and flare
        Above a wondering earth.

In vain the hilltops hearken,
        Their lips no sound reveal;
But ever on, from arc to arc,
Across the spangled depths of dark
        Their pennons whirl and wheel.

Why come they? Who can answer?
        Whence go they? Who can tell?
Flaming and fading down the night,

THE WIZARD PEOPLE

A mystery, a dream-delight,
    A splendor and a spell!

Such are the wizard people,
    The brethren of the pole;
And though man long has sought to gain
Their secret, suns shall wax and wane
    Ere he shall read their soul!

HOLLY SONG

C are is but a broken bubble,
       Trill the carol, troll the catch!
       Sooth we'll cry, "A truce to trouble!"
Mirth and mistletoe shall match!

Happy folly! we'll be jolly!
       Who'd be melancholy now?
With a "Hey, the holly! ho, the holly!"
       Polly hangs the holly bough.

Laughter lurking in the eye, sir,
       Pleasure foots it frisk and free;
He who frowns or looks awry, sir,
       Faith, a witless wight is he!

Merry folly! what a volley
       Greets the hanging of the bough!
       With a "Hey, the holly! ho, the holly!"
Who'd be melancholy now?

GENNESAR

Bright 'neath the Syrian sun, dim 'neath the Syrian star,
   Thus lieth Galilee's sea, sapphirine lake Gennesar;

Girdled by mountains that range purple and proud to their crests,
Bearing the burden of dreams,—glamour of eld,—on their breasts.

Just one white glint of a sail dotting the brooding expanse;
Beaches that sparkle and gleam, ripples that darkle and dance;

Grandeur and beauty and peace welded year-long into one,
Under the Syrian star, under the Syrian sun!

And over all and through all memories sweet of His name
Kindling the past with their light, touching the future with flame!

FIRELIGHT

Whene'er at evening on the pictured wall
I watch the flickering firelight rise and fall,
From out the shifting shadow-vistas come
The forms of those who marched to martyrdom,—
Unflinching souls no agony could tame,
A martyr wraith for every tongue of flame!

MOTHER-OF-PEARL

Mother-of-pearl out of Bethlehem,
　　　　Irradiant with all rainbow lights,—
　　　　Shimmering, shifting opal whites,
The June-time rose's palest fire,
The sunset's most translucent gold,—
Delicate as a precious gem
Shaped for a lover's heart's desire,
Glowing as morn, yet virgin cold!

Mother-of-pearl out of Bethlehem,
Thus I read you, bending above
Your sheen, more fair than the breast of a dove;—
The white is the Mother without a stain;
And the blended hues, the fire and the gold,
They stand for Him who for diadem
Had a crown of thorns, and was basely slain,—
The Son of God clad in mortal mould!

THE BELLS OF ARDO

By wide gray orchards girdled,
    And cloistered deep in vines,
    Remote stood ancient Ardo
Amid the Apennines.

Below her banded belfries
    That loomed above the land
For weeks gaunt Plague and Famine
    Had walked with linkèd hand.

Until, when neared the Yule-tide,
    On pale lips swooned the prayer,
And only sounds of wailing
    Swept down the bitter air.

No heart had any ringer
    To sound the joyful bells;
The soaring campanile
    Pealed naught but burial knells.

THE BELLS OF ARDO

So when the Christmas sunlight
    Scattered the chill white haze
The sorely scourgèd people
    Were smitten with amaze

Hearing from San Stefano,—
    A spire and shrine forlorn,—
A glorious jubilate
    Salute the startled morn.

Fast flocked the folk, and wonder
    Swelled high that dawning hour,
For unseen hands were swinging
    The bells within the tower.

And 'twixt their rhythmic chiming,
    Word upon precious word,
A vibrant voice of promise
    In solemn wise was heard;

"This day," it cried, "my people,
    The cruel curse shall cease,
And there shall fall upon you
    My benison of peace!"

When failed the silvery bell-notes
    Till arch and aisle were still,
'Twas found that all in Ardo
    Were healed of every ill.

And now, as Christmas morning
    Breaks over street and square
The bells of San Stefano
    Ring out upon the air;

THE BELLS OF ARDO

And still the gathered people
    Lift praise with glad accord
Unto the One almighty
    That was their fathers' Lord.

IN THE AGE OF THE YEAR

Is it the wizard wind
    That has shriveled the quince's rind?
    Sooth, we know it was he
Who shook the leaves from the tree
And danced them out of breath
Till they wizened away in death!
Strange and subtile powers
Have rule of these ashen hours,
Binding the stricken sphere
In this, the age of the year.

Through the crispèd grass and the husk
Rustle the feet of the Dusk;
And the only song we know
Is the back-log's murmur low.
Then come, and sit with me
By the side of Memory
And Love, with the bluet skies
In her spring-reverting eyes,
And there shall be vernal cheer
In this, the age of the year!

A LOVER'S CHRISTMAS

Fade the last embers in the year's chill urn;
    Ah, love, how red the holly berries burn!

A shroud of ermine hides the meadow ways;
Ah, love, how green are still the ivy sprays!

Black are the boughs against a sky of gray;
Ah, love, how golden is the Yule-log's ray!

Behind the wood the sad wind plaineth long;
Ah, love, the mirth within the mummer's song!

In garth and orchard naught but gloom and dearth;
Ah, love, the joy about the Christmas hearth!

Winter's white woe, its bitter sting and smart—
Ah, love, the love aye vernal, in the heart!

BALLAD OF KIRKLAND HILLS

The grand old hills of Kirkland
    Stood up against the morn,
  As o'er a rutty road there strode
A pilgrim lean and lorn.

The wood-crowned hills of Kirkland,
    They notched the wan blue sky,
As toward that plodding pilgrim came
    A horseman urging by.

"I prithee, weary pilgrim,
    Now whither dost thou roam?"
"I seek a gabled farmstead set
    Amid these hills of home;

"I seek an ancient rooftree set
    Amid these uplands white."
"God give thee luck," the horseman cried,
    "Before this Christmas night!"

BALLAD OF KIRKLAND HILLS

The kindly hills of Kirkland,
    They saw, when broad noon shone
Above the fair Oriska vale,
    This pilgrim toiling on.

The hemlocks preened their night-dark plumes
    As up and up he clomb;
The same old rook-calls welcomed him
    Back to the hills of home.

High on the hills of Kirkland
    Where hale the north-wind roared,
O gay were they that grouped about
    The heapèd Christmas board!

And yet the brooding mother,
    With smiles she hid the tear
For one whose lips she had not kissed
    This many a lonely year;

For one whose wander-lust had led
    His roving spirit far,
Until she dreamed he slept beneath
    The clear Alaskan star.

Hark, at the door a summons!
    A step upon the sill!
O mother-eyes abrim with joy,
    And mother-heart athrill!

And O ye hills of Kirkland,
    In wintry white and gray,
A gladder sight ye never saw
    On any Christmas day!

THE CLOSED ROOM

In the marvelous house of life
    Each year is a closèd room;
  It is filled with peace and strife,
  It is packed with glow and gloom.

There are hopes in the hues of dream,
    There are cares in their grim array,
There are pleasures that glint and gleam,
    And sorrows in drugget gray.

For some, with his infinite grace,
    Love waits when the portal jars;
For some, with his sphinx-like face,
    Death stands when the door unbars.

Some back from the threshold shrink,
    As loath from the past to part;
But the most plunge over the brink
    With never a fear at heart.

THE CLOSED ROOM

Then silent closes the door
    At the sound of the last old chime,
And the key—Forevermore—
    Is turned by the keeper—Time!

UNDER THE HOLLY BOUGH

When the hale year laughed in the prime of May,
    And each path was a lure to the truant eye,
    When the south-wind sang: "Come away! Come away!"
      (Ah, but the blue of a vernal sky!)
    When the vireo's voice was a lyric cry,
'Twas the bloom o' the apple beckoned us; now
    When we meet, my sweet, for the trysting, why,
'Tis under the green of the holly bough!

When the meadows swooned in the dazzling day,
    And the hilltops seemed in a dream to lie,
When shrill was the locust's roundelay,
      (Ah, but the glow of a summer sky!)
    When the stream-song sank to a rippling sigh,
'Twas the pleach o' the elm-leaves beckoned us; now
    When we meet, my sweet, for the trysting, why,
'Tis under the green of the holly bough!

UNDER THE HOLLY BOUGH

When the woodland gleamed like a prismy ray,
    And the distance drowsed in a golden dye,
When vineyard and orchard aisles were gay
    (Ah, but the depths of an autumn sky!)
    With stains like a web of Tyrian ply,
'Twas the flame o' the maple beckoned us; now
    When we meet, my sweet, for the trysting, why,
'Tis under the green of the holly bough!

ENVOY

    Spring, summer and autumn have all sped by,
    (Ah, but the chill of a winter sky!)
    Yet love still calls to the tryst, and now
    'Tis under the green of the holly bough!

COSETTE'S CHRISTMAS

Cosette they called her; Cosette, that was all;
    Fragile she was and flower-like, slim and tall
    For her eleven years, wherein her heart
Had known but little save the world's sharp smart.
Never her ear had heard a mother's croon;
Never for her, about the break of June,
Had been outstretched a father's shielding hand
To guide her woodward through the smiling land.
The streets oppressed her with their cruel roar;
The birds she saw above her dart and soar,
Theirs was the life she longed for, not to be
Mewed within walls that were a gloom to see,
And stung with taunts from a virago tongue
That aged her spirit yearning to be young.
Foundling,—a fate that brooked of no appeal
Was hers by some inexorable seal.

Backward and forward oft she went and came
From the grim spot, that was but home in name,
On casual errandry. It chanced one day,

COSETTE'S CHRISTMAS

As she passed swiftly on her timid way,
('Twas near the season of the Christ-child's birth,
The happy tide of peace and love on earth)
A heedless hand struck from her feeble grasp
The glass she strove so carefully to clasp,

And she beheld it, with a plaintive cry,
Shattered before her on the pavement lie.
The throng swept by, and caught her in its swirl;
There was no lip to soothe the sobbing girl,
No kindliness to aid her. A great fear
Clutched at her breast; she knew the stabbing jeer,
The pitiless blows that waited her when she
Told the ill outcome of her errandry.
Then through her brain there flashed a sudden word
That in the hive-like purlieus she had heard,
And filled her mind with sunshine. No affright
Touched her with chill at thought of death's dim night,
For she recalled how once the preacher said
That in white lily-gardens walk the dead.
So in she stole at the accustomed door,
Sought out a room upon the lower floor
Wherein the porter, sullen-visaged, slept;
Toward a remembered drawer on tiptoe crept,
Plucked, undetected, thence a shining thing,
And gained again the street in triumphing.
A ringing shot, a little piteous moan,
And a child's blood encrimsoning the stone!
When Cosette oped her heavy-lidded eyes,
Wonder assailed her, and a great surmise.
Was this the lily-land of her delight?
It shone so bare, and yet so very white!
Long stainless walls and little cots in rows,
And one whose smile invited to repose;
She drowsed, her mind still dwelling on that face,
And dreamed she'd found the angels' sleeping-place.

COSETTE'S CHRISTMAS

And when, next day, they told her where she lay,
A tiny tear-drop found its mournful way
Adown the death-like pallor of her cheek;
She closed her eyes and sighed, but did not speak.
Dawn followed dawn, and still the little one
Went not to that dim bourn beyond the sun,
But ever seemed about to pass thereto;
Nearer and nearer now the Yule-tide drew,
And to the hospital one morn there strayed
A kindly man who made the news his trade,
And learned the piteous story of the maid.
"Cosette," he said, with a strange catch of tone,
His sight grown dim, remembering his own,
"Have you no wish?" and she, with him at ease,
Cried,—"Two red roses and an orange, please!"

Just two red roses and an orange! So
He wrote next day that all the town might know;
Then Christmas morning broke above the snow.
The morn of Christmas broke; bell spoke to bell
The loving message of "good-will" to tell;
The postmen bustled on their burdened round;
And happy greetings rang with cordial sound.
Then, at the hospital, a summons came,
Another and another, and the name
The answering nurse with every message met

Was still "Cosette," and evermore "Cosette,"
For all had read the story of the child.
Roses upon her bed were strewn and piled,
And breathed their June about her everywhere,
Gleamed on the table, glistened on the chair,
From the soft loveliness of the pale tea-rose
To the deep splendor of the Jacqueminots.
And oranges! forsooth, it was as though
The palm-set lands where the long trade-winds blow,
Fair Florida and the Lucayan shores,

84

COSETTE'S CHRISTMAS

Had here unbosomed their most precious stores!
Both rich and poor had sought to ease the smart
Of her whose tale had touched the city's heart.
And she—Cosette—through kindness' golden dower,
Smiled upon life, and mended from that hour.

PILGRIMS

Their path who shall unravel,
      Their purpose who unroll?
  From out the past they travel,
  The future is their goal.

Theirs are the forward faces,
      The spring's Arcadian airs;
The old eternal graces
      Of youngling Time are theirs.

Or gold the sky or ashen,
      There broods within their breast
The sleepless pilgrim passion,
      The sweet divine unrest.

They neither flag nor falter,
      They tarry not nor tire;
Their aim they will not alter
      Although a king desire.

PILGRIMS

They fear nor frost nor fever,
 Nor fire nor famine they;
They follow Fate, the weaver,
 For ever and a day.

Now tell their eyes the story
 Of more than mortal tears,
Now gleam with starry glory,
 The passing pilgrim Years.

Copyright © 2022 by Alicia Editions.
Credits: www.canva.com
All rights reserved.
No part of this book may be reproduced in any form or by any electronic or mechanical
means, including information storage and retrieval systems, without written
permission from the author, except for the use of brief quotations in a book review.

www.ingramcontent.com/pod-product-compliance
Lightning Source LLC
LaVergne TN
LVHW092008090526
838202LV00001B/47